I am a Soul I am a Soul I am a Soul I am a Soul I am a Soul

I am a Soul I am a Soul I am a Soul I am a Soul I am a So
I am a Soul I am a Soul I am a Soul I am a Soul I am a S
l I am a Soul I am a Soul I am a Soul I am a Soul I am a
ul I am a Soul I am a Soul I am a Soul I am a Soul I am a
oul I am a Soul I am a Soul I am a Soul I am a Soul I am
Soul I am a Soul I am a Soul I am a Soul I am a Soul I am
Soul I am a Soul I am a Soul I am a Soul I am a Soul I a
a Soul I am a Soul I am a Soul I am a Soul I am a Soul I
a Soul I am a Soul I am a Soul I am a Soul I am a Soul I
m a Soul I am a Soul I am a Soul I am a Soul I am a Soul
am a Soul I am a Soul I am a Soul I am a Soul I am a Soul
am a Soul I am a Soul I am a Soul I am a Soul I am a Sou
I am a Soul I am a Soul I am a Soul I am a Soul I am a So
I am a Soul I am a Soul I am a Soul I am a Soul I am a S
l I am a Soul I am a Soul I am a Soul I am a Soul I am a
ul I am a Soul I am a Soul I am a Soul I am a Soul I am a
oul I am a Soul I am a Soul I am a Soul I am a Soul I am
Soul I am a Soul I am a Soul I am a Soul I am a Soul I am
Soul I am a Soul I am a Soul I am a Soul I am a Soul I a
a Soul I am a Soul I am a Soul I am a Soul I am a Soul I
a Soul I am a Soul I am a Soul I am a Soul I am a Soul I
m a Soul I am a Soul I am a Soul I am a Soul I am a Soul
am a Soul I am a Soul I am a Soul I am a Soul I am a Soul
am a Soul I am a Soul I am a Soul I am a Soul I am a Sou
I am a Soul I am a Soul I am a Soul I am a Soul I am a So
I am a Soul I am a Soul I am a Soul I am a Soul I am a S
l I am a Soul I am a Soul I am a Soul I am a Soul I am a
ul I am a Soul I am a Soul I am a Soul I am a Soul I am a
oul I am a Soul I am a Soul I am a Soul I am a Soul I am
Soul I am a Soul I am a Soul I am a Soul I am a Soul I am
Soul I am a Soul I am a Soul I am a Soul I am a Soul I a
a Soul I am a Soul I am a Soul I am a Soul I am a Soul I
a Soul I am a Soul I am a Soul I am a Soul I am a Soul I
m a Soul I am a Soul I am a Soul I am a Soul I am a Soul
am a Soul I am a Soul I am a Soul I am a Soul I am a Soul
am a Soul I am a Soul I am a Soul I am a Soul I am a Sou
I am a Soul I am a Soul I am a Soul I am a Soul I am a So
I am a Soul I am a Soul I am a Soul I am a Soul I am a S
l I am a Soul I am a Soul I am a Soul I am a Soul I am a
ul I am a Soul I am a Soul I am a Soul I am a Soul I am a
oul I am a Soul I am a Soul I am a Soul I am a Soul I am
Soul I am a Soul I am a Soul I am a Soul I am a Soul I am
Soul I am a Soul I am a Soul I am a Soul I am a Soul I a
a Soul I am a Soul I am a Soul I am a Soul I am a Soul I
a Soul I am a Soul I am a Soul I am a Soul I am a Soul I
m a Soul I am a Soul I am a Soul I am a Soul I am a Soul
am a Soul I am a Soul I am a Soul I am a Soul I am a Soul
am a Soul I am a Soul I am a Soul I am a Soul I am a Sou
I am a Soul I am a Soul I am a Soul I am a Soul I am a So
I am a Soul I am a Soul I am a Soul I am a Soul I am a S
l I am a Soul I am a Soul I am a Soul I am a Soul I am a
ul I am a Soul I am a Soul I am a Soul I am a Soul I am a
oul I am a Soul I am a Soul I am a Soul I am a Soul I am
Soul I am a Soul I am a Soul I am a Soul I am a Soul I am
Soul I am a Soul I am a Soul I am a Soul I am a Soul I a

TILLING THE SOUL

AURORA PRESS

TILLING
THE SOUL

Published by
Aurora Press
205 Third Avenue, 2A
New York, N.Y. 10003
First Printing: 1984

Book Design: Adrian Taylor,
Teresa Murphy
Cover symbol of the Soul:
Alden Cole, Wingate
Typography: Cosmos
Communications, Inc.
Carnase Typographers
Letterform design: Carnase, Inc.
Production Consultants:
William S. Konecky
Associates

With special thanks to Allan Richards

To my beloved Emmanuel,
who is not only my teacher,
but my dearest friend
and partner also.

May I show forth our light,
     our love, our joy and our purpose
in all my doings
          throughout each day.

TiLLING THE SOUL

PART 2: THOUGHTS SHARED WITH THE COMMUNION OF SOULS AFTER MEDITATION

PART 3: TOOLS AND PRACTICES

Introduction

No one has ever called me a Perfect Master.

Nor do I go around claiming to be Enlightened.

But I've studied with good teachers.

I've done my homework. I practice what I teach.
And I'm growing.

In **Tilling the Soul,** I share with you my growth
practices and the basic tools I use, along with some of
the fruits of my gardening.

Perhaps these tools and these practices
of mine will help you in cultivating the garden of your
own consciousness, as they have already helped
me and many others who have studied with me here
at the Communion of Souls.

And perhaps my truths and realizations,
and that's all they are, **my** truths and **my** realizations,
will help you discover the same truths and realizations
developing unnoticed within **you**.

Perhaps show you what you
already know but don't yet know that you know.

And if all my truths are not your truths and
all my realizations are not your realizations, then put
those of mine that are not also yours in some far
corner of your garden for awhile and then see how
you feel about them later.

Or cross them out and use them as
compost to stimulate the growth of truths and
realizations that **are** right for you, and then use the
blank pages to write them down.

In this way your copy of **Tilling the Soul**
will become a combination of spiritual journal,
growthbook and ongoing record of your progress
along the winding path to Soul Consciousness.

Usuigato

January, 1983

5

PART

1

TRUTHS
AND
REALIZATIONS

The Age of the Soul

We are standing on the threshold of an exciting and challenging new age, the **Age of the Soul.**

Of the Soul becoming conscious of Itself.

The Age of the Guru, of the Master, of the feeling that only by sitting at the feet of another could we find our truths and realizations, is only now winding down after more than two thousand years.

And along with this, the much more recent Age of Reason, of feeling that science and knowledge would give us our answers, is winding down also.

In the new Age of the Soul we will find our answers deep within ourselves. And we will find our happiness and our fulfillment there also, instead of outside ourselves where we have been looking so unsuccessfully for so many lifetimes.

TILLING THE SOUL

In other words, we will stop looking in all the wrong places and we will stop chasing all the wrong rainbows as well.

In the new Age of the Soul we will seek first Soul Consciousness, secure in the knowing that all else will inevitably follow.

We will become **Tillers of the Soul.**

Which doesn't mean that Tilling the Soil won't still be important to us. Earning a living, having a career, raising a family and things like that will always have their place.

But none of this needs to get in the way of Tilling the Soul. As a matter of fact, Tilling the Soil and Tilling the Soul work very well together. They actually complete and complement each other.

We become more conscious by growing taller, not by detaching from the soil and floating around in mid-air. The soil is where our roots are, and it's important for us to keep grounded, much as a tree keeps grounded by growing deeper and stronger roots to support its ever increasing height.

TILLING THE SOUL

THE AGE OF THE SOUL

It's just that as we become more
Soul Conscious, Tilling the Soil will become
less important to us and Tilling the Soul more and
more important, until one day we will realize that it
has become our Number One priority.

And then? Then we will be chasing the right
rainbow at last, the one with the pot of golden light
waiting at the end of it.

The Flowering of
Soul Consciousness

Before a plant can bear flowers,
it needs to have roots and branches and leaves, with
each growing out of the other while at the same
time continuing to grow with the other.

So it is with our Consciousness, with Its roots
going back to a very Simple Consciousness. This is
the kind that everything has. Plants have it. The cells
in our bodies have it. Even rocks have it.

This is the Consciousness of primitive man. Of
Adam and Eve before the apple. Of each of us when
we were very young, and it has its advantages. We are,
but we don't know that we are. There is no sense of
Self, of I am. No I am good, no I am bad. No guilt. No
shame. No I am naked, where's a fig leaf.

Then there are the branches and leaves
of Self-Consciousness, or Consciousness of-Self, of I
am, of me, me, me, and this is where we are now.

We've eaten the green and bitter apple
of opposites. We're out of the garden and into the
jungle of good and bad, of love and hate, of success
and failure. Of judgment. And guilt.

We're separated and apart, fighting
and struggling to get more and more so we can have
enough, and to become better and better so that
we **are** enough in the endless pursuit of our
lost happiness.

It's been hard and unpleasant work. But
it's also something we all have needed to grow
through. And for many of us it's almost over.

The Age of Soul Consciousness
on a truly planetary scale has finally come.

And with Its flowering there will be an end of
opposites. There will be no more love and hate. Only
love. No more joy and sorrow. Only joy.

No more good and bad. Only good,
and a sense of the Divine Perfection of all things.

There will be no more fighting and
struggling. Only a sense of partnership and
cooperation in an unfolding Plan.

TILLING THE SOUL

SOUL CONSCIOUSNESS

There will be no more judgement. Or guilt.

There will be no more feeling separate
and apart. Only a feeling of oneness, within ourselves,
and with every one and every thing.

There will be abiding happiness. There
will be the love that passeth all understanding. And
there will be an understanding of the meaning
and purpose of life.

We will be back in the Garden again,
realizing that we never really left It. That It is the
world around us. And that the only thing that has
changed is ourselves.

We started off being totally innocent,
and we have ended up becoming totally conscious.

We finally realize it all. We realize that
the One Soul is not outside us, as we believed for so
many lifetimes. We realize that It is not just tucked
away somewhere inside us either. We realize at last
that It is in us as us.

We realize that we and the One Soul are One.

TILLING THE SOUL

The Anatomy
of the Soul

The Soul is a body of glowing, incandescent light pervading and permeating Its physical body. Even extending beyond it. And just as the physical body has its different organs like the heart and the brain and the liver, so the Soul has Its different Centers of Consciousness.

There are seven of these Centers of Consciousness. The 1st of them is located in the area between the sex and the base of the spine. The 2nd at the sex itself. The 3rd in the belly. The 4th in the heart area. The 5th in the throat area. The 6th in the area of the brain. And the 7th extending beyond the top of the head.

These seven Centers are capable of expanding and contracting. As they expand, they tend to overlap and blend, especially the 1st and 2nd Centers, and the 6th and 7th Centers, which are very close to each other.

TILLING THE SOUL

Each of these seven Centers has Its own quality of Consciousness and Its own way of experiencing.

Yet one Center is not better than another. A higher vibration, yes. Like purple has a higher vibration than orange. And G on the musical scale a higher vibration than C.

But better? Is purple a better color than orange? Or G a better note than C?

Just as the artist needs all of the seven colors to paint his masterpiece, and the composer needs all of the seven notes to write his symphony, so we need **all** of our seven Centers, fully developed and fully conscious, to become Soul Conscious.

True Alchemy and the Three Essential Growth Energies

We're all going to become Soul Conscious sooner or later. We can't help it. It's what evolution is all about.

But it can be a lot sooner than later if we will start doing a better job of providing the Soul with the three essential energies It needs for Its growth.

The first and by far the most important of these energies we call the Soulfire. This is the catalyst for our becoming more conscious.

And although there is an endless supply of this primordial essence buried deep within our 1st Center, Its flame is burning very, very low and our growth has therefore been very, very slow.

TRUE ALCHEMY

In order to speed things up, we need to get the Soulfire burning hotter and brighter. This we do with the second of these energies, the Life Force, which we use to feed and fan the flame of the Soulfire as if It were a kind of spiritual oxygen. We also use the Life Force to purify and strengthen our different Centers of Consciousness so they can safely handle the increased amount of Soulfire that is generated.

And then finally there are our Experiences. They are fuel for our growth, but for us to really learn from our experiences we need to burn them in the sacred flame of the Soulfire. For only in the fertile ashes that result can a new and higher Consciousness spring up.

In other words we need to practice True Alchemy, which is not transmuting base metals into gold, but transmuting Self Consciousness into Soul Consciousness.

It is our Soulfire Meditation.

TRUE ALCHEMY

The secrets of True Alchemy have been
known through the ages by a special few, hidden away
behind the closed doors of Mystery Schools and
Spiritual Centers around the world.

But this is the Age of the Soul and of
Soul Consciousness for the Many and not just for
the Few. And those secrets are no longer behind
closed doors but out in the open and available
to the many of **us** who are now ready to make them a
part of our lives.

A Cosmic Seed Catalogue

What happens as we transmute Self Consciousness into Soul Consciousness, and how fast it happens, differs somewhat within each Soul. But eventually there are important and dramatic changes in the Consciousness of each of our seven Centers and it helps to have a clear vision, like a kind of Cosmic Seed Catalogue, of what this new Consciousness will be like.

For example, we're not nearly so concerned with security, things like our basic need for food and shelter which were so important and all-consuming for primitive man and still preoccupy so many of us.

We're secure in the Universe now, and that is enough.

We're secure with our sexuality also.

We don't have to repress it anymore. There's no need to. The energy isn't bottled up in our 2nd Center the way it used to be, but instead is flowing freely to all our Centers.

TILLING THE SOUL

And when we want to express our sexuality,
we can do it with our total beingness and not with just
a small part of us.

It has finally become the wondrous gift it
was always meant to be. Not the physical joining of
two bodies, but the blending of two Souls.

It has become true Soul Mating.

And our negative emotions and our driving
need to always come out on top that used to boil
and bubble away in our 3rd Center are no longer
around to torment us either.

They're gone. Dissolved. Washed away.
Because the resistance to "what is" that caused
them in the first place is gone.

Without resistance to "what is" there
are no more negative emotions. Just love and
happiness. And compassion.

And without this resistance we have
nothing to prove, nothing to become, except what
we already are.

Soul Realization and a Whole New Sense of I Am

As the alchemical process continues and the buds of Soul Consciousness that have been lying dormant in the 4th and 5th and 6th Centers are quickened by the warmth and light of the Soulfire, there is Soul Realization and a whole new sense of I Am.

I Am conscious of My Self again after having buried this awareness in my humanness for many, many lifetimes.

No longer am I conscious of being just a person, a man or a woman named so and so, who is married or divorced or single, a butcher, a baker, a candlestick maker, with a body that is male or female, tall or short or fat or thin, with eyes of one color, hair of another, and skin of another, that was born and will eventually die.

I Am also a Soul.

Not I **have** a Soul, that's part of my old realization, but I **Am** a Soul.

I Am a Mind. A Consciousness.

I Am created, not born. I have lived before the birth of my physical body, and I will live after its death. For me there is no death. Only life.

I think. And feel. And will. And my human manifestation, with its brain and body, is but my instrument which I use to express the Unfolding Plan and to experience the lessons I came into this life to learn.

I Am a body of glowing, incandescent light. I Am energy. And, like all the other energies, I Am both positive and negative, male and female, not more one than the other but a perfect blending of the two, complete and whole within myself.

Because I Am still human, I Am still in time. But I Am also beyond time in the timelessness of the infinite and the eternal, and this brings me a new perspective and a whole new way of experiencing as well.

There is a special Meditation Practice in Part Three called **The Practice of Being a Soul** that will help you to develop Soul Realization.

Soulmates

In the past, before Soul Consciousness
and the Soul Realization that goes with It, we felt
a very strong identity with our male or female physical
bodies. And, if we thought about the Soul at all, It was
usually as something we had that was either male
or female also.

In either case we felt uncomfortably incomplete
and put a great deal of time and energy into seeking
completion and wholeness outside ourselves in
someone else.

And if and when we found someone, especially a
special someone, we would often think of ourselves as
being Soulmates.

But True Soulmates are not two half-souls or
half-bodies that are drawn to each other, as we so
often were, out of need or frustration or loneliness
or fear.

True Soulmates have already found their
completion and their wholeness within themselves,

and when **they** come together it is not out of need or of lack but in richness and in fullness.

It is not to complete one another but to enhance one another.

True Soulmates are already happy and loving. Their lives already have meaning and purpose. And they bring all this **to** the relationship instead of expecting to take it **from** the relationship.

Gone is the need to belong to one another. To cling. To bind. To hold on to each other.

Instead, True Soulmates enrich each other by having a single life as well as a shared life.

By drinking out of each other's cup instead of the same cup.

And the best part of all this is that Soul Realization, which is such an essential ingredient in being a True Soulmate, is happening to more and more of us everyday.

TILLING THE SOUL

Flowing Acceptance

As the buds of Soul Consciousness that have been lying dormant in our 4th and 5th and 6th Centers are further quickened by the warmth and light of the Soulfire, there is Flowing Acceptance.

It is the centerpiece of our Cosmic Seed Catalogue and with Its realization there is an entirely new and exciting way of experiencing.

For example, we feel an abiding happiness that wells up from deep within us and has nothing to do with what happens **to** us.

We are no longer happy because or unhappy because. We are happy period.

We feel a love that passeth all understanding, and like our newfound happiness, it too wells up from within us.

It is **unconditional** love and it has nothing to do with what someone else is or isn't, or does or doesn't.

TILLING THE SOUL

And we understand the meaning and purpose of our life. Even more important, we understand that our life has meaning and purpose.

And what that meaning and purpose is.

With Flowing Acceptance I certainly feel a happiness that I never felt before.

I realize that what I have is enough. That it is all I need to have, here and now, to take the next step on my path.

I realize that what I am is enough. That it is just the way I need to be, here and now, to take that step.

And I realize that life is not a fight to test me but an experience to teach me, and that I am constantly being provided with just what I need for my growth.

So I'm happier here with what I have. I'm happier now with what I am. And I'm happier with my life and where I am on the trip.

And before Flowing Acceptance there was no real happiness.

TILLING THE SOUL

No matter how hard I worked to have more
so that I could be happy with what I had, I never quite
had enough.

More this. More that. Or a different this or
a different that. There always seemed to be the need
for something more or something different.

And no matter how hard I worked to become
more so that I could be happy with what I was, I could
never quite **be** enough.

Before Flowing Acceptance there was no real
love, either. No matter how hard I tried to be really
loving, I just couldn't love the way I wanted to love.

There were always those warts of imperfection
on other people's noses. Worse still, there were all
those warts on my own nose. And on my work. And
on everything around me.

But now, with Flowing Acceptance, I realize that
Perfection is not the way things **should** be but the way
things actually are.

That Perfection is never finished, never complete,
but always growing. Like a perfect seed growing into a
perfect flower.

TILLING THE SOUL

FLOWING ACCEPTANCE

Like Omega* is growing. Not from "imperfection" to Perfection, but from Perfection to Perfection to Perfection.

And I realize that everyone and everything are part of this Perfection. That the Universe is part of It. The world is part of It.

The warts are part of It.

I am part of It. I am just the way I'm supposed to be. Just the way Omega wants to be. In me. As me. By accepting this I can accept myself, and by accepting myself I can love myself as well.

My neighbors are part of it. By accepting this, I can accept my neighbors and love my neighbors also. Which is not the same thing as liking them. Or wanting to be with them.

And with Flowing Acceptance I realize that there is only good. There is only Omega. And that bad is how I see those experiences whose part in my growth I do not yet understand.

By accepting this, I can accept my life and all it brings me, and love my life as well.

And isn't loving myself and loving my neighbors and loving my life and all it brings me the only way to truly love Omega?

---

* Using Omega as my name for the One Soul has helped free me from a lot of old, wornout concepts. God, for example, can only be male, while there is no reason why Omega can't be both male and female.

yes, my

In order to love Me, you first must love yourself.

For I am in you as you, and whatever you are,
I AM. You are part of My Perfection.

And how can you love Me, My Beloved,
except that you love yourself?

And second, My Beloved, you must love your
neighbors.

For am I not your neighbors also?

And are your neighbors not also part of
My Perfection?

Beloved

And finally, My Beloved, you must love your
life and all it brings you. Not only what you call
good, but also what you call bad.

For am I not everyone and everything. Both what
you call good. And what you call bad?

Only by understanding this and loving both can
you truly love Me.

And how can you love yourself, My Beloved,
but by loving Me? For are you not in Me as Me, as
I am in you as you?

Are we not One?

And with Flowing Acceptance and the Consciousness that goes with It I can see that life does have meaning and purpose.

That **my** life has meaning and purpose, that it is going somewhere, that it is directed, while before Flowing Acceptance there seemed to be only senseless fate and chaos.

Now I see that there is an ordered Universe with an Unfolding Plan, and that It is Perfect.

That there is a Divine Will that is the dynamic energy behind this Plan.

And that it is through this Will that Omega is expressing Itself.

And through Its Surrender that Omega is experiencing Itself.

And I see that it is through **my** will that I am expressing Omega and Its Unfolding Plan. And that it is through my surrender that I am experiencing It.

I see that this **accepting** the Plan, this **opening** to It, is the only kind of surrender* I ever need to make.

---

* Not the surrender of the 3rd Center, where surrender means throwing up your hands, waving a white flag, giving up, but the surrender of the 4th Center, where it has an entirely different vibration.

It is no longer giving up. It is opening up. And experiencing.

And that the Will to flow with the Plan, to cooperate with It, to help bring It into being, is the only Will I ever need to have.

Yet accepting the idea of Flowing Acceptance and wanting to help it grow wasn't all that easy for me.

It sounded too much like resignation, like giving up, like the opposite of fighting. And that's not the way I was brought up. I was brought up to be a fighter, to be aggressive, to win.

But I finally got it through my heart that Flowing Acceptance is not the opposite of fighting at all. It's not the opposite of anything.

Fighting is like swimming against the current, struggling with it, opposing it. And its opposite is floating, letting the current carry me like it carries a dead leaf, getting caught up in an eddy and endlessly going around in circles.

But Flowing Acceptance is not floating. It is swimming, like fighting is swimming. But it is swimming **with** the current, not against it.

It is accepting the current and whatever it brings me, and at the same time It is flowing with it, using its energy, cooperating with it and fulfilling it in a perfect blending of Will and Surrender.

There is a special Meditation Practice in Part Three that will help you develop Flowing Acceptance.

What About Free Will?

Free Will and Flowing Acceptance just don't belong in the same garden together and it's time for Free Will to go and good riddance.

It may have been a beautiful flower once in the wild rebellious days of our spiritual adolescence, but It's only a weed now, a flower in the wrong place, and It's getting in the way of our growth.

With Free Will there is no sense of cooperation or partnership with some Unfolding Plan like there is with Flowing Acceptance. There is no The Will, The Plan, Our Way.

Instead Free Will is separation and apartness. It is all me, me, me. My will, my plan, my way. My choice. With Free Will that is how we grow. Through choice. And life is but a cosmic maze filled with the skeletons of all our past mistakes.

While with Flowing Acceptance we don't need choice anymore. That's no longer how we grow. We grow now through experience, and life is

not a maze but a winding path, filled with just the experiences we need for our growth and leading us inevitably to our goal.

Free Will isn't all that free either. There's a lot of guilt that goes with it. And anguish and anxiety and questioning and doubt. Why did I do this? Why didn't I do that? And on and on and on.

It's Flowing Acceptance that is really free. Certainly we're free from guilt and doubt and all those other negative emotions. They're gone, along with our age-old resistance to the Unfolding Plan.

And it turns out that Free Will is a fraud and a delusion after all.

That it is always the One Will in us that willeth, and Free Will is but a lower vibration of the One Will, perfectly expressing Itself and Its Unfolding Plan. In us; and through us.

And we cooperate with the One Will just as much with Free Will as we do with Flowing Acceptance.

The big difference is that with Flowing Acceptance we are able to express a much higher vibration of the One Will.

And do a much better job of showing forth Its Light. And Love. And Joy. And Purpose.

The New Laws
of Manifestation

In the dark, unlighted days of Self Consciousness
and Free Will we were taught that "I am the Master of
my fate, the Captain of my soul, in total and complete
control of my life", and that with the right thoughts
and enough belief, expectancy and desire and a few
simple techniques we could get whatever we wanted
to have or wherever we wanted to go.

Sometimes we did. More often we didn't, and
then there were the inevitable feelings of frustration
and failure and inadequacy and lack.

But with Flowing Acceptance and Its
total surrender to the Unfolding Plan and Its total
commitment to bringing the Plan into being, we see
the Laws of Manifestation and how they work in
an entirely new and different light.

No longer are they to control or attract.
Or fill a need. We have no need that is not already
being perfectly met by the Unfolding Plan.

THE NEW LAWS OF MANIFESTATION

Instead, we use the Laws, if we use them
at all, to fulfill that Plan. Or at least that part of It that
wishes to express itself in us and through us.

And we use the Laws, not with tension
or anxiety or fear of "failure" or expectation of
"success", but with love, and gratitude, and joy in
being a conscious partner in the divine process.

Omega Realization

And finally, as the Consciousness of our 7th Center comes into flower, we begin at last to realize it all.

We realize that we are a body, but that we are more than a body. That we are a human being, a person, but that we are more than that. That we are a Soul, but that we are more than just **a** Soul.

We begin to realize that we are joined in the most deeply intimate communion with every other Soul in the Cosmos. That we are joined with the One Soul. That It is in us, as us. That we and the One Soul are One.

And we begin to realize who and what the One Soul really is.

No longer are we bogged down by the teachings and dogmas of an age when it was believed that the Universe was only 3000 years old and 3000 miles in diameter.

TILLING THE SOUL

Now we are free to experience the One Soul
in whatever way It needs to manifest Itself to **us,** in
whatever way It needs to reveal Itself to us, for us to
be able to understand It and accept It.

And it doesn't seem to matter whether this
happens through revelation, or realization, or listening
to the still small voice within. Or by just feeling as
though we were "making it up".

Each has played its part in the past. Each
is a valid way of getting our own answers to the age-
old question of who and what the One Soul really is,
and as an example of how this can work for you I have
jotted down on the next page or two what the
One Soul is to me.

"Call Me Omega"

Or God, or Jehovah, or Brahma, or Allah, or anything else you would like to call Me.

I AM all of these. Yet I AM also none of them.

I AM the Cosmos, the Universe. Everything That Is.

I AM the Chaos, the Void. Everything That Isn't.

I AM the First Cause.
I AM the Last Effect.
I AM Every Cause and Every Effect.

I AM Spirit.
I AM Soul.
I AM Matter.

As Spirit, I AM the inexpressible, indefinable Source of All Being, infinite and eternal.

As Soul, as Spirit manifest for an Evolution, I AM Mind. I AM Consciousness. I AM Beingness.

And as Matter, as Soul manifest for a lifetime, I AM Everyone and Everything.

I AM Perfect, and Every Cause and Every Effect and Everyone and Everything are Part of My Perfection.

I AM THE ONE.

I AM ALSO THE MANY.

AND WHATEVER IT IS THAT SAYS I AM, I AM **THAT** I AM.*

---

* Imagine Omega pointing at someone or something while saying **THAT.**

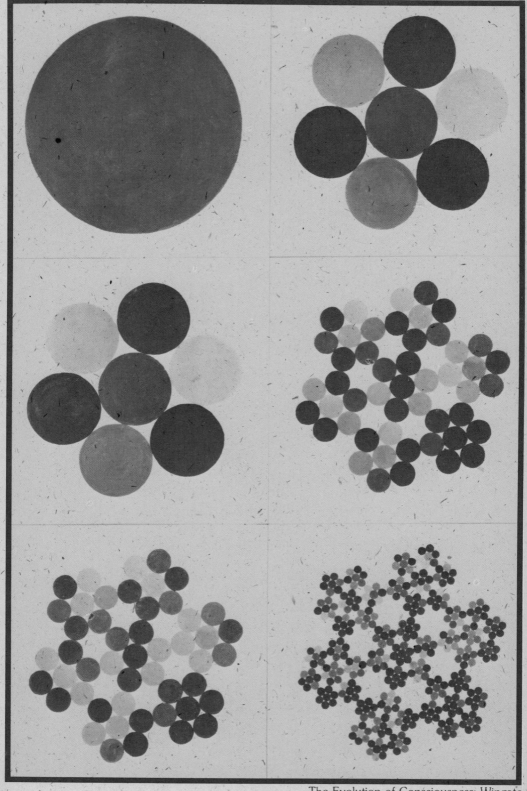

The Evolution of Consciousness: Wingate

Beyond
Soul Consciousness

If the One Soul, the One Mind, the One
Consciousness became the Many, in us as us, and is
now becoming the One again, and if we are becoming
the One again, how is this all going to happen?

Will there be instant Oneness, once we become
Soul Conscious? Or will there be a continuation of our
evolutionary growth of the past.

Did the One Soul become the Many
by dividing Itself into smaller and smaller Souls, and
are these Souls now blending and merging and
becoming the One again.

Will I blend and merge and become one
with other Souls. And is this how I continue to grow
and become more conscious.

But what happens if I keep on blending and
merging and blending and merging. Does my one
drop of Consciousness become forever lost in the
great ocean of the One Consciousness?

Do I become less and less until finally I become Nothing. Is that what happens. Is that the way it will all end for me: Is that what growth is all about?

Or do I become more and more until finally I Am the Ocean?

Do I, and Everyone and Everything, separately and together and without any loss of I AM, become the One Consciousness. The One Mind. The One Soul?

OMEGA.

On Becoming a Christ,
Or a Buddha

Isn't it time to stop being a Christian, or a Jew, or a Buddhist, or an atheist, or whatever we are, and to start becoming a Christ? Or a Buddha?

Isn't this what Jesus was teaching his disciples? Not the basic dogma and theology of Christianity, but how to become like Him? And have His Consciousness?

And was Gautama teaching His devotees Buddhism? Or was He teaching them how to become Buddhas, and have Buddha Consciousness?

Down through the centuries there have always been a special few who have had Christ Consciousness, or Buddha Consciousness, or Soul Consciousness. They're all basically the same thing.

But today this is happening much more frequently. And isn't this what the Age of the Soul is all about?

Not the coming of Jesus again, or Gautama again, but the coming of Their **Consciousness**? And not just to the Few, but to the Many?

And finally to THE ALL?

A Summing Up

We are each of us a Soul.
A Mind. A Consciousness. A Body of glowing,
incandescent Light.

We are both male and female, complete and whole
within ourselves.

Yet we are also joined in the most deeply intimate
communion with every other Soul in the Cosmos.

Omega, the One Soul, the One Mind,
the One Consciousness became the Many and is
now becoming the One again.

We are becoming the One again.

Omega is perfect, and we are part of Its Perfection.

We are just the way we need to be, just the way
Omega needs to be, in us as us, to take the next step
on our path.

We have just what we need to have, just what
Omega needs to have, to take that step.

And Life is constantly providing us with just
what we need to experience, just what Omega needs
to experience, along the way.

There is only good. There is only Omega.
Bad is how we see those experiences whose part
in our growth we do not yet understand.

It is all part of the Plan, and we are partners
in Its unfolding.

PART
2

THOUGHTS SHARED WITH THE COMMUNION OF SOULS AFTER MEDITATION

TILLING THE SOUL

Thoughts Shared

My first experience with Flowing
Acceptance happened early one winter morning in
1973. I was getting ready to take a shower and
wondering how I was going to make it through the
horrendous day I had looming ahead of me feeling the
way I did, when a little voice asked me if I could
handle taking a shower feeling the way I did,
and suggesting that sufficient unto the moment was
the good thereof.

It startled me, because I wasn't used to
hearing little voices. But it also seemed like a
reasonable suggestion, so I took my shower and found
myself no longer thinking about what was ahead
of me but just enjoying my shower and feeling
better moment by moment.

And that's how I went through what turned
out to be one of the truly memorable days of my life,
one flowing, accepting step after another.

TILLING THE SOUL

23 September 1982

Years ago, I had a teacher who used to talk about someday having a saffron-colored Rolls Royce.

The Rolls Royce part I could understand. After all didn't every guru worth his salt have at least one. But the saffron-colored part. That puzzled me.

When I finally got up the courage to ask him why saffron, he smiled and then explained that saffron was the color of Renunciation. And that he didn't really want a Rolls Royce, certainly not a saffron-colored one, but that it was a good way to get me thinking about possessions and attachment.

And then he went on to explain that **having** possessions was not the problem. Money was not the root of all evil as the Bible is so often misquoted as saying, but the **love** of money. And you could give away everything you had and still be attached to your begging bowl.

In other words, have any thing you want, including a saffron-colored Rolls Royce. Just don't be attached to it.

4 October 1982

Do we really own our possessions. Do they really belong to **us,** or are they only in our custody for as long as we need them.

And if they are only loaned to us, don't we have a responsibiity to take good care of them, not because they are "ours" but so they can be of service to someone else when they are no longer of use to us.

14 October 1982

Celibacy is supposed to be very spiritual.

But ask ten people what celibacy is and you will get ten different answers. Because celibacy is no sex, and it is very hard to find agreement on just what sex is. Or isn't.

What about kissing, for example. Is that sex? Or hugging or holding hands. Or just looking deep into another's eyes and feeling very much one with them.

Or being joined in the most deeply intimate communion with another Soul. Or being joined with every other Soul in the Cosmos?

In other words, is sex just the joining together
of two physical bodies, or is it any act that brings us
closer to a state of oneness with another, whether it be
the first glance across a crowded room or the ultimate
union with Omega.

But even if we think of sex only in its most
limited sense, isn't the whole concept of celibacy, even
at this level, a denial and a repression of something
that is very important to our growth, since we need all
our Centers of Consciousness, the 2nd no less than
the 7th, fully evolved and fully developed if we are to
become Soul Conscious.

On the other hand, the more we get into
Tilling the Soul, the more important it becomes for us
to expose ourselves to vibrations that are positive and
nourishing, rather than those that are negative and
damaging to the good vibrations that we have worked
so hard to develop.

And in the case of sex, because we are
usually very open and vulnerable and the vibrations
very strong, it is particularly important for us to be
discriminating and avoid those relationships which
could be harmful to our growth.

Which could very well mean that there will
be times when it will serve us better to be celibate than
go to bed with the wrong vibration and be sorry.

11 November 1982

A teacher needs to be used, like a cow needs to be milked. We all need to be used. We all need to be milked.

If we aren't, if we aren't given an opportunity to do our thing, whatever it may be, we become frustrated and in great pain, like a cow with a full udder.

What we don't want is to be used badly, to be taken advantage of. But even this can sometimes be better than not being used at all.

22 November 1982

Soul and Mind and Consciousness, as in "I Am a Soul, a Mind, a Consciousness, a Body of glowing, incandescent Light" are three ways of saying pretty much the same thing.

For example, according to Webster's Dictionary the Soul "is credited with the functions of thinking and willing and hence determining all human behavior; the emotional nature of man".

Mind is "that which thinks, feels, wills; the seat of consciousness".

And Consciousness is "the totality of one's
thoughts, feelings, impressions; mind".

So when Descartes, the great French
philosopher, wrote his famous words "I think,
therefore I am" wasn't he expressing only a part of
our total Beingness?

I think, therefore I am what? Some kind
of cold and calculating machine? Certainly not a Soul
or a Mind or a Consciousness that not only thinks
but feels and wills as well.

Let Descartes speak for Descartes. For me, "I think,
I feel, I will, therefore I Am" says it a whole lot better.

16 December 1982

Planet Earth is really a School of Higher
Consciousness in disguise, and we are all of us
struggling students in It.

Classrooms come in all sizes in this
cosmic School of ours, the hours are long and
the vacations short, and the list of subjects available
is almost endless.

Some, like "Raising Healthy Happy Kids" and "Making Your First Million", are still very popular but others, like "Living a Meaningful Life" and even "Tilling the Soul" are beginning to attract attention.

But in order to graduate and get a Masters Degree in Soul Consciousness, each of us, without exception, will have to successfully complete the course in "Advanced Flowing Acceptance".

And after graduation from Planet Earth? Is that the end of our education? Or is there another school to go to somewhere else and a PhDeity in Omega Consciousness to look forward to?

30 December 1982

I gave up on Will Power a long time ago, but I had to go through a lot of failed resolutions and unfulfilled vows before I realized that It just wasn't working for me.

And it wasn't too hard to figure out why. By Its very definition Will Power meant not doing something I very much wanted to do, or doing something I very much didn't want to do, and neither one lasted for more than a few weeks.

TILLING THE SOUL

And besides, if I had to make a resolution
or take a vow to give something up, didn't that mean
that I wasn't finished with It yet? That It still had a
lesson to teach me?

So I decided to go with Want Power instead, and
that always, or almost always, works. And why not?

After all, don't we always do what we want to
do. And don't we do it with an irresistible enthusiasm
and commitment to succeed that is just the opposite of
the gritting-the-teeth kind of determination that makes
using Will Power so unpleasant and so ineffective.

Next time you decide to make a resolution
or take a vow ask yourself if it's something you really
want to do. Deep down.

If it's not, forget it and save yourself a lot of
grief and guilt. And if it **is** something you really want to
do, then tell yourself that it is. Over and over and over.
I **want** to do this and because I want to do it I will do it.

17 January 1983

In India they catch monkeys by cutting a small
hole in a gourd, just big enough for a monkey's hand
to slip through, and putting some food inside.

No monkey can resist reaching in and grabbing
the food, and of course when it does its clenched fist is
too big to pull back through the hole again.

So there the monkey is, stubbornly holding on to
the food that isn't doing it a bit of good, until someone
comes along and puts it in a sack, while all the time it
could have gotten free just by letting go.

It's a sad little story but aren't we all of us, each in
our way, desperately holding on to something that we
really don't need.

And unable to take the next step on our path
because of it.

17 February 1983

That wart on the end of my nose that you find
so disturbing, you know why it bothers you? Because
it reminds you that you have the same kind of wart on
the end of your own nose.

It's as though I were a mirror, and everything
you see in me that you dislike or that rubs you the
wrong way is only a reflection of something in yourself
that you have not yet accepted.

So please accept yourself and love yourself just as you are, warts and all. For only by doing this can you accept my warts and truly love me also.

28 February 1983

Service, as in "Serving Mankind", is a very tricky concept.

Do doctors serve their patients by helping them get well? Or do patients serve their doctors by being sick.

Do teachers serve their students, or do the students serve their teachers.

Or do cows serve the farmers by giving milk, or do the farmers serve their cows by milking them and providing them with food and shelter.

The answer of course is that everyone and everything, doctors, patients, students, teachers, cows and farmers are all serving the Unfolding Plan, whether they are conscious of it or not.

And there are as many levels of **Conscious** Service as there are levels of Flowing Acceptance, and with Full Flowing Acceptance and a total commitment to serving the Unfolding Plan, a life of Pure Service is possible.

It is not for everyone to become an Albert
Schweitzer or a Mother Therese and go to Africa or
India to take care of the sick and the hungry.

Each of us has been given our own part of the
Plan to fulfill and our own part of the world to do it in.

But if we are filled with Full Flowing Acceptance,
if we are totally surrendered in our hearts to the One
Will and totally committed to consciously bringing Its
Plan to fruition, then we are living a life of Pure Service
no less than they.

24 March 1983

I know that the Lord loveth a cheerful giver,
and that it is supposed to be more blessed to give than
to receive.

But it's also a whole lot easier and more
satisfying to be a cheerful giver and have someone
beholden to us because we have in some way done
them a favor.

It's much more difficult to ask for help, or
a favor, when we need it. And even more difficult
than that to be a genuinely grateful receiver when
our needs are met.

And saying thank you just doesn't express it. True gratitude comes from the heart, not the lips, and the best way to express it is to show it in the eyes. And to use whatever has been given to us well, and with caring.

With all the cheerful givers there are in the world, there just aren't enough grateful receivers to go around.

And I'm sure the Lord loves grateful receivers just as much and they will be just as blessed as the cheerful givers.

14 April 1983

The Affirmation of Soul Consciousness that seems to give the most trouble is the one that says there is only Good.

In a world of holocausts and the bomb and cancer such a statement seems totally outrageous.

But remember, this is the way a fully realized Soul sees things and an affirmation such as "there is only good, there is only Omega" is only a step on the path to such realization.

TILLING THE SOUL

Until you complete the transition from Self
Consciousness and Its world of good and bad to Soul
Consciousness, there will always be things that don't
make any sense. That seem just plain bad, bad, bad.

But remember also that bad is only how you see
those things whose part in **your** growth you do not yet
understand, so don't set yourself up as a judge of
what's good or bad for someone else's growth.

Instead, look back over your own life and ask
yourself if there is anything that has happened to you
that didn't serve your growth and therefore have
good in it.

And, although it may not have seemed that
way at the time, if that is true of the past why is it not
also true of the present, and why not get in the habit of
looking for the good in whatever is happening to you
right here and now.

25 April 1983

How can you be sure there is a Cosmos and not
a Chaos? That there is an Unfolding Plan? That the
Universe is directed and is actually going somewhere?

You can't really. It's impossible to be completely sure about things like that. Show me someone who **is** and I'll show you a fanatic, and I'm not comfortable with fanatics. They like to burn people at the stake.

Even St. Paul cried out in the agony of his doubting, "I believe; help Thou mine unbelief".

And an extraordinary minister named Samuel Shoemaker once said to me that he found it "just that much easier to believe in God," holding his thumb and forefinger only a quarter of an inch apart, than to not believe in Him.

Dr. Sam was a great preacher, and I've always felt that this was his finest sermon.

I believe in a Cosmos. A Chaos just doesn't make sense to me, not even "that much".

And if it turns out there is a Chaos after all and my beloved Cosmos was only a bad, bad joke?

That's always a possibility, of course, But at least in the meantime my life will have been filled with meaning and purpose, and a joyous sense of being a partner in an Unfolding Plan.

Soul Realization is another one of those seeming paradoxes we run into so often in this kind of work, because becoming Soul Realized is simply a matter of allowing ourselves to be what we already are, just as we are, warts, clay feet and all those other things that go into being human.

And only when the Soul is acknowledged in its physical manifestation can You in Your humanness become a realized instrument for Its spiritual expression.

So instead of striving to be a Soul by becoming spiritual, why not do it the other way around and allow the Soul to be human, in you, as you. As is.

26 May 1983

Gautama, the Great Buddha, was born with a golden spoon in his mouth, but in his twenties he gave it all up, palaces, servants, beautiful women, you name it, to go on a spiritual quest that eventually led Him to the very heights of Soul Consciousness.

In the process, no one ever meditated more, or fasted more, or worked harder than Gautama, but His progress seemed to be frustratingly slow.

One evening, weak and emaciated from His efforts and finding He could barely pull Himself out of a little stream where He had been bathing, He flopped down in utter exhaustion and complete despair and decided once and for all, that's it, I've had it, and I quit.

And at that moment His heart opened in total surrender and what He had been seeking for so long happened and He was enlightened.

Which doesn't mean that Surrender is the Path to Soul Consciousness.

Surrender **is** Soul Consciousness.

And the path to Surrender is the path of will, of self will and free will, with all the frustrations and failures and little surrenders that go with them.

And the last step on that path is giving up whatever is left of our little wills and completely surrendering **in our hearts** to the One Will and Its Unfolding Plan.

Which doesn't mean we will be will-less. Not at all. We will be filled to overflowing, as Gautama was, with the gentle power of the **One** Will. And be partners at last in the conscious expression of Its Divine Purpose.

TILLING THE SOUL

16 June 1983

Omega is not just sitting somewhere in a lotus position and watching all that goes on in our lives as a compassionate observer.

When the One Soul became the Many, It buried Its Consciousness in each of us in order to experience what it was to be human.

And now in the Age of the Soul and of the Soul becoming conscious of Itself again, the One Soul is also becoming conscious of **Itself** again, in us as us, and this is what we call Omega Realization.

27 June 1983

Light is most needed where there is darkness. And there is a much greater need for those of us who live and work in the dark corners of our planet to show forth our light than there is for those who live where there is a great deal of light already.

So why not get in the habit of lighting the candle of love and joy and meaningful purpose during meditation each morning and taking it out into the world with you.

And don't for one moment think that your light may not be bright enough to be meaningful. In darkness the light from even a single match can be enough to show the way.

7 July 1983

If there's an Unfolding Plan and life is all predetermined anyway, why shouldn't you pick up and go off to the South Seas and spend the rest of your life in a hammock sipping long cool drinks?

Well, for at least two reasons. First, because you would probably be bored to distraction in two months.

But second, and far more important, because that doesn't seem to be part of your Unfolding Plan. If it were, you would probably already be on your way.

19 July 1983

Letting go of the conscious control of your life is like letting go the tiller of a boat and allowing it to set its own course.

It's hard to do when you have a specific harbor you are struggling to reach, and are sailing in the well-charted waters of Self Consciousness and anxiously know where all the rocks and shoals are.

It gets a lot easier as you reach the relatively uncharted, unsailed seas of Soul Realization and Flowing Acceptance, where it doesn't much matter whether you have the tiller in your hand or not.

You don't know where you're going anyway, and you don't know where the rocks and shoals are either.

But there's no anxiety anymore. Just a quiet curiosity as to where the wind and waves of the Unfolding Plan are carrying you, and a clear willingness to cooperate with them in any way you can to get there.

4 August 1983

It used to bother me a lot that I couldn't hear "the still small voice within". I felt very deprived.

But I felt a lot better about it after talking with a dear friend named Eileen Caddy who is one of the founders of Findhorn, a world-renowned spiritual community in northern Scotland.

Eileen has been hearing **her** still small voice ever since a memorable visit she made years ago to Glastonbury Abbey, and so it was especially reassuring to have her tell me that I really didn't need to hear a voice the way she did..

That that wasn't the only way it worked, and that anyone could get guidance that would be just as valid and just as true by listening to their intuition and their deep sense of inner knowing instead.

PART

3

TOOLS
AND
PRACTICES

Meditation and
Its Practice

Meditation is not so much an act of doing as It is a state of being. Of being totally and completely aware of the doing, whatever it is.

It is fully experiencing each experience, whether it's sitting in a lotus position watching a candle flame or washing the dishes, and this here and now state of awareness is your basic, all-purpose gardening tool, not only for Tilling the Soul and growing Soul Consciousness, but for Tilling the Soil as well.

It will make everything you do more meaningful and more effective, whether it is working with the Soulfire and the other essential Growth Energies, or working at your job, or just playing a game.

But if you are like me when I first started, you're not all that used to being in this here and now state of meditation and you're going to need to practice it. Which won't take time away from living

your life, because you will be practicing with things you do every day anyway.

Like breathing, and walking, the two Meditation Practices that Gautama was supposed to have taught his followers.

The Breathing Meditation can be done anywhere, sitting at your desk, standing in line, riding on a bus or a train, or just taking a break between chores.

To make it a Meditation Practice, just become aware of your breathing, of the movement of your belly as you breath in and out. It's that simple. And then for however long you decide on, five minutes, ten minutes, see how much of that time you can be aware of just your breathing and nothing else.

The Walking Meditation is practiced in much the same way, only now your whole awareness is focused on the movement of your feet.

Some of you may prefer to practice this in a room or a garden like the Buddhist monks do, just barely moving the feet. The slow motion may help you focus your awareness.

Others of you may prefer going outside and really striding along, or even jogging.

But of course anything and everything you do can be used as a Meditation Practice, and it doesn't really matter which ones you choose so long as they work well for you.

The ones that work best for me, besides the Breathing and Walking Meditations, are the Soulfire Meditation and the Practices of Being a Soul and Flowing Acceptance.

And then there are others like driving a car, preparing a meal, listening to good music, working in the garden, and thinking the thoughts that go into **Tilling the Soul**.

But thinking can get in the way of any Meditation Practice. And for a very good reason. You just can't fully experience more than one thing at a time. You can't think and fully experience what you're feeling, for example. Or what you're hearing. Or seeing, or smelling, or tasting.

And yet you have thoughts going on in the background of your awareness almost constantly. And the more noise there is from your thoughts the less you can experience. But it works the other way around too.

The more you experience, the less noise
there is from your thoughts. And if you are truly in a
meditative state, there isn't any noise at all. Any
thoughts at all.

So it looks like thoughts are going to
have to go. Which won't be any great loss,
because most of your thoughts are just meaningless
chatter about experiences you've had in the past, or
about experiences you may have in the future, and
have very little to do with what's going on in your life
here and now.

And those that do are too important to only half
think, but instead deserve your full attention like any
other Meditation Practice.

Being in a here and now state of Meditation
means breaking the habit patterns of a lifetime and it's
not going to happen overnight. But it can be done
with practice, and the rewards will be well worth
the time you put into it.

The Practice of Being A Soul

Once you begin to realize that yes, you are indeed "a Soul, a Mind, a Consciousness, a body of glowing, incandescent Light" and that you are "both male and female, complete and whole within myself", it is time to start cultivating this Soul Realization by making it one of your regular Meditation Practices. It has certainly become that for me.

But in the beginning I had difficulty identifying with that male and female body of glowing incandescent Light, so I worked out a special Soul Visualization Meditation to help me come up with a Soul image that would be easier for me to identify with. Then I put It on tape and played it back while I followed the guidance of my own voice.

This worked very well for me, and if you are having a similar problem you might like to do the same thing, using the same Meditation that I used.

If you do decide to make your own tape, familiarize yourself with the Meditation before you

start recording it. And don't be surprised if you come up with one or two images while you are doing this. Just don't reject them, they could be important. But don't cling to them either. The main thing is to be open and receptive during the Meditation Itself.

Once you begin recording, give yourself a minute or two at the beginning of the tape to do the Breathing Meditation Practice. And be sure to allow enough time between paragraphs for you to experience whatever is happening.

Then start reading aloud the words in quotation marks.

"Allow an image that symbolizes your female or male* Soul aspect to emerge from you. Imagine it happening, even if you feel you are making it up."

Imagination is an essential tool for attuning to any higher, unseen vibration and it should be used with confidence and trust. And when you feel as though you are just imagining something, as though you are just making it up, then ask yourself why you are making **that** up instead of something else.

---

* Read either ''female'' or ''male'', not both. If you are a woman, it would probably be easier for you to start with your female Soul aspect that your male one, and if you are a man it would probably be the other way around.

"Take time to become aware of this image, what it looks like, how you feel about it.

"Now merge with this image, blend with it, identify with it. Experience what it is like to **be** this image, to have it in you as you.

"Now allow this image to move out of you and experience it being outside of you again.

"Now allow an image that symbolizes your male or female* Soul aspect to emerge from you. Imagine it happening, even if you feel that you are making it up. Take time to become aware of this image, what it looks like, how you feel about it.

"Now merge with this image, blend with it, identify with it. Experience what it is like to **be** this image. To have it in you as you.

"Now allow this image to move out of you and experience it outside of you again.

"And now have the two images begin to relate to each other. Observe what they are doing. Listen to what they are saying.

---

* Again read just one or the other. If you read "female" the first time, then read "male" this time and vice-versa.

Be aware of how you feel about what is happening.

"Now see them moving closer together. Blending.
Merging. Becoming One.

"Take time to be with this image and to explore
what it is like. Be aware of how you feel about it.

"Now blend with this image. Identify with it.
Experience what it is like to **be** this image. To have it
in you as you.

"Now practice **being** this image. Practice being
a Soul.

"And then, whenever you are ready,
open your eyes, holding on to the feeling of being a
Soul for as long as you can."

If you had difficulty visualizing a blended and
merged Soul image, then you could practice being
either your feminine or your masculine Soul aspect,
and practice the **presence** of your other Soul aspect.

Imagine it being with you, beside you, a
companion, a partner, someone to talk with,
to walk with, to be with.

Soon you will find yourself reversing roles,
and then it won't be long before you will be happily
practicing the presence of both Soul aspects in
you as you.

Finally blending and merging and becoming One.

The Practice of Being a Soul, can be a Meditation
Practice all by itself. Or it can be combined with other
Meditation Practices.

For example, the Practice of Being
a Soul is a valuable way to begin the Soulfire
Meditation, involving as it does Energies and Centers
of Consciousness that are all part of the
Soul vibration.

As a matter of fact, it's a good way to start any
Meditation Practice. You are a Soul, and it is You who
think and feel and will, and Your human manifestation
with its brain and body is but Your instrument,
which You use to express the Unfolding Plan and
to experience the lessons You came into this life
to learn.

THE PRACTICE OF BEING A SOUL

So practice thinking as a Soul, feeling as
a Soul, **willing** as a Soul. And walking and breathing
and whatever else you do **as a Soul**.

It will change your life. If nothing else, you
will be much more involved in the journey and much
less concerned about getting there.

The Practice Of
Flowing Acceptance

Flowing Acceptance is the most beautiful and important flower in the whole garden of Soul Consciousness and, once It has begun to blossom, Its development can be encouraged and intensified through regular practice.

My own experience has been that the best practices are those that are very structured and physicially oriented, otherwise the whole concept of Flowing Acceptance tends to become vague and formless and very difficult to get a handle on.

One such practice that I have used often is in the form of a simple ceremony in which I imagine stepping stones around a circle in my Meditation Room where each step brings me closer and closer to the center.

This is my special place of Flowing Acceptance, and once I reach it I sit and go over any recent events in my life and open to them and whatever they are trying to teach me as best I can.

Then I attune to that space deep within me where all that is knowable about the Unfolding Plan is already known and flow with whatever guidance is being offered me.

Another Flowing Acceptance Practice that has served me very well is the practice of accepting and flowing with Time.

Whenever I become aware of the time, and with all the clocks and watches around this happens very often during the day, I surrender to the reality of the time, whether it is convenient or not.

And then I flow with the time, relaxing into it and, without rushing or becoming frantic, doing whatever I need to do to fulfill the purpose of the moment.

In the beginning, this was difficult for me, very difficult. Like most of us, even those who pretend Time doesn't exist, I was really a slave of Time, and it took a lot of practice before I was able to break free of Its chains.

And a lot of reminding myself whenever I got uptight about being late that getting somewhere or doing something on time wasn't nearly as important in Omega's Timeless Universe as practicing and learning Flowing Acceptance.

Another Flowing Acceptance practice that I use often is singing row, row, row your boat gently down the stream, merrily, merrily, merrily, merrily, dee, te dum, te dee.

This is the way Flowing Acceptance should be. Just **gently** rowing, cooperating with the current, with the Unfolding Plan, and helping to fulfill Its Purpose.

Down the stream, **with** the current, not against it. No struggle. No outthrust jaw. No gritting the teeth.

And **merrily**. Especially merrily. With a song, perhaps this song, in your heart. You might even want to incorporate it into your various Meditation Practices, singing it at the end lightly and softly and at the same time going through the motions of gently rowing while you imagine the current carrying you along.

And no steering. Just a letting go of the need to control the direction of your life and instead allowing the current to carry you wherever it wants to take you.

But whether you use my practices or develop your own, keep them structured and physically oriented.

And keep them as light and as joyous as you can because that is what Flowing Acceptance is all about.

The Soulfire
Meditation

The Soulfire Meditation doth make alchemists of us all. It is the magical tool I use to transmute the darkness of Self Consciousness into the glowing, incandescent Light of Soul Consciousness, and over the years It has served me and many others very well indeed.

There are 10 Steps to this most important of our tools and practices, some of them with roots going all the way back to Padmasambhava, founder of Tibetan Buddhism.

The 1st Step is to get into a good position. The 2nd is to establish Your basic breathing rhythm. The 3rd is to relax Your physical body. The 4th is stilling Your thoughts and calming Your emotions. The 5th is cleansing and strengthening and vitalizing Your Centers of Consciousness.

THE SOULFIRE MEDITATION

The 6th Step is feeding and fanning the
flame of the Soulfire. The 7th is to bring the Soulfire
to each of Your different Centers of Consciousness.
The 8th is affirming the Soul quality of each Center
of Consciousness. The 9th is to repeat the Ten
Affirmations of Soul Consciousness. And the 10th
Step is Singing the Song of the Soul.

And from the very beginning remember
to practice being a Soul. To practice realizing as best
You can that You are a Soul and that it is You who is
doing the Meditation. That it is You whose Centers of
Consciousness are being transformed. And that it is
You who thinks and feels and wills and directs Your
physical instrument in whatever way is necessary for it
to serve Your purpose.

STEP 1 OF THE SOULFIRE MEDITATION

The First Step of the Soulfire Meditation is to get into a good position, which means getting into a position that allows the Soulfire to flow freely to Your different Centers of Consciousness, as well as one that Your physical body can hold without moving or feeling discomfort during the full thirty minutes that the Soulfire Meditation takes.

So be sure that You are sitting erect but without strain. The Soulfire uses a channel in the spine and the straighter You sit the easier You make it for the Soulfire to flow. And sitting erect is also the most comfortable way to sit.

If on a chair, sit on the front edge with both feet planted on the floor and hands on the thighs, palms up.

If on the floor, which is where You will probably feel best, You will need at least two or three pillows to start with. Again sit on the front edge, this is very important, and tuck one heel, usually the left, against the crotch **and** the bottom pillow. Then bring the right foot in front of the left, or place it on top of the left thigh and again rest Your hands on Your thighs, palms up.

Be sure You aren't sitting on Your spine the way You are used to. If You are, just bring the weight forward until it is more evenly distributed between Your buttocks and Your legs.

Both knees should now be firmly on the floor, otherwise the entire weight of Your legs will be pressing on the small bones of Your feet and Your ankles. But if they aren't on the floor, don't push down on them. Just add pillows until they are. With practice You will probably find Yourself using fewer pillows, but the number of pillows You use has nothing to do with how spiritual You are.

If You turn out to be one of those who want to sit on the floor but who can't comfortably do so, even after weeks of practice, try a seiza or kneeling bench. It's simple to use. Just kneel on the floor, slide the bench under You and then sit down.

If there's no place to buy one where You live, You can easily make one, or have one made. The one we use here at the Communion of Souls has a tilted seat that is 16" long and 6" wide, with two legs that are 6" high in front, 7½" high in back and the same width as the seat.

But whether You sit on the floor or use a kneeling bench or sit on a chair it is essential, if the Soulfire Meditation is to be effective, that You maintain a firm but relaxed posture with the spine straight, the head erect and shoulders down.

TILLING THE SOUL

STEP 2 OF THE SOULFIRE MEDITATION

The Second Step of the Soulfire Meditation is to establish Your Basic Breathing Rhythm. But before you begin, be sure You are breathing properly, the way singers and actors are taught to do, and the way we all did when we were babies.

Take a minute now to become aware of what Your physical body is doing as You breathe in and out. Especially Your diaphragm. Is it expanding as You breathe in, and contracting as You breathe out? Or is it doing just the reverse, with Your chest doing all the work.

The first way is belly breathing or right breathing, and if You found You weren't doing it, here's how You can get back to the way You used to breathe as a baby.

Start by exhaling. Bring the belly in against the spine. Don't suck it in. Push it in. Then inhale by letting the belly expand. This will bring all the oxygen You ordinarily need into Your lungs.

For a normal breath there is no movement of the chest. Just the belly. The chest is used only for a very deep breath, and then only as the last thing You do. But whether You breathe normally or deeply, You will never hyperventilate breathing this way.

If you have difficulty getting back into belly breathing, lie down and relax and You will find it happening quite naturally.

Once You have mastered this belly breathing, start breathing in and out to a regular count. Breathe out. Then breathe in, smoothly and steadily, to a count of 4. Breathe out, again smoothly and steadily to a similar count of 4, continuing this rhythmic breathing, counting more slowly as You quiet down and get more centered, until each complete 8 count takes about 10 seconds.

This Basic Breathing Rhythm, combined with good, strong Belly Breathing, is such a basic part of the Soulfire Meditation that I urge everyone who comes to the Communion of Souls for study and meditation to practice it in a good sitting position at least ten minutes a day for a week before going on to the other 8 Steps.

TILLING THE SOUL

STEP 3 OF THE SOULFIRE MEDITATION

It is important to have a relaxed physical body before starting Your work with the Growth Energies. It serves no purpose to intensify the flame of the Soulfire, for example, and at the same time block its flow with tension, and Step Three of the Soulfire Meditation is to relax your physical body.

The best way to relax is by first being aware, by experiencing, not by falling asleep. A good way to start is to focus Your awareness on the top of Your head. Become aware of a warmth there, or a tingling sensation. Feel it relaxing. Still maintain Your Basic Breathing Rhythm while You do this.

Then allow this feeling of warmth and relaxation to flow slowly down to Your forehead. Feel the furrows smoothing out.

To Your eyelids. Unclench them and open them just slightly. But not enough to let in light if Your eyes are kept directed slightly above the horizontal.

To Your cheeks. Your jaw. To Your mouth. And Your tongue. Which is usually rammed into the roof of Your mouth or against Your front teeth. You don't need it there except to swallow. Instead, get in the habit of carrying it away from Your teeth and at the bottom of Your mouth. Do it now and experience what happens.

To Your throat. You probably felt it relax as soon as You relaxed Your tongue.

To Your shoulders. Don't round them forward. But don't have them hunched up around Your ears either.

To Your arms. And Your hands. Relax Your chest area. And finally Your abdominal area.

Be sure as You continue with the Soulfire Meditation, that tension doesn't creep back in, especially in the shoulders and throat, and that your eyes are looking up above the horizontal and your tongue is down.

STEP 4 OF THE SOULFIRE MEDITATION

The Fourth Step of the Soulfire Meditation is to still Your thoughts and calm Your emotions, and they can get in the way of the Growth Energies just as much as physical tension. A good way to do this is to become totally absorbed in Your Basic Breathing Rhythm.

The more aware You are of Your breathing, the less aware You will be of Your thoughts. And Your emotions. You have probably experienced this already if you have been practicing Your Basic Breathing Meditation.

If You are really being torn apart by worry, or anger, or fear, or anxiety, it's probably better not to attempt to do the Soulfire Meditation. On the other hand, the slow, steady belly breathing of Your Basic Breathing Rhythm will work wonders because it's just the opposite of the rapid, irregular high-in-the-chest breathing that goes with emotion.

Just be sure You are focusing on the rising and falling of Your belly, and not on why You are worried, or angry, or frightened, or full of anxiety. That only adds fuel to the fire. And any answer You come up with probably won't be the right one anyway.

You'll make much more sense, and do whatever You have to do better, if You can wait until You've calmed down.

STEP 5 OF THE SOULFIRE MEDITATION

The Life Force, or spiritual oxygen, is brought to Your Soul Body in much the same way that regular oxygen is brought to Your physical body. When You breathe, You are not just breathing oxygen, which cleanses and vitalizes the physical body. You are also breathing the Life Force, which cleanses and vitalizes Your Soul Body.

You do this all the time without thinking about it, just as You breathe regular oxygen without thinking about it either. But in the Soulfire Meditation You do think about it. You do it consciously. And because of this You do it better.

You begin working with the Life Force by breathing It in and out of Your 4th Center three times, holding the third inbreath for an extra count of 4. Breathe It high up into Your nose, with nostrils slightly flared and tongue relaxed.

Follow It as It travels down behind Your tongue and the back of Your throat to Your 4th Center.

As You exhale, and be sure to do this with emphasis, imagine* the Life Force flushing out any toxins and poisons that have accumulated there.

On the second inbreath, feel Your 4th Center expanding and filling with more Life Force than It did with the first one. With the outbreath continue the cleansing process.

On the third and last inbreath, which You hold for an extra count of 4, feel Your 4th Center expanding to Its utmost. Feel the Life Force strengthening It. And vitalizing It. Then exhale strongly and steadily, flushing out the toxins and waste one more time.

Breathe the Life Force in and out of Your 3rd Center in the same way. Then Your 2nd Center. And finally Your 1st Center.

Practice doing this a few times before going on to Step Six.

---

* Throughout the Soulfire Meditation You will be using Your imagination as you did in the Soul Visualization Meditation, only now You will be using it as a way of attuning to the higher, inner vibrations of the Life Force and the Soulfire and Your Seven Centers of Consciousness.

TILLING THE SOUL

STEP 6 OF THE SOULFIRE MEDITATION

In many ways the Soulfire, buried deep within Your 1st Center, is like any other fire. For example, It doesn't burn very well if it doesn't get enough oxygen. And for It to burn with the kind of flame You need if You're to really grow, It's going to have to get a lot more Life Force, or spiritual oxygen, than It's been getting so far.

You do this by continuing to breathe the Life Force in and out of Your 1st Center. But You do it now with a new purpose and a new image of what's happening. Instead of doing it to expand and strengthen and cleanse Your 1st Center, You now do it to feed and fan the Flame of the Soulfire. And because energy follows thought, that's all there is to it.

As You breathe in, imagine the Soul Fire smouldering at the core of Your 1st Center. Then imagine It burning brighter and the flame growing larger as You bring It more and more of the Life Force.

THE SOULFIRE MEDITATION

As You breathe out, do it strongly, almost explosively, using Your belly like a great bellows directed towards the Soulfire. Imagine the flame flattening and spreading out from the force of Your outbreath.

Continue feeding and fanning the flame of the Soulfire as You breathe in and out until You can sense It filling Your 1st Center with Its warmth and light.

The Soulfire has been getting to Your different Soul Centers all along without Your doing anything special about It. It hasn't been getting there very well, but It's been getting there. And It's been doing the best It can to transmute Your Experiences into a new and higher Consciousness.

But now that the Soulfire is burning so much better than It was before, and there is so much more of it available, it only makes sense to further intensify the alchemical process by starting to bring It to Your different Centers of Consciousness **consciously**.

You do this by again changing the focus of Your awareness. Now, instead of concentrating on bringing the Life Force **down** with each inbreath as You have been, You concentrate on drawing the Soulfire **up**.

And don't be concerned about how the Soulfire gets to each Center. Supposedly It goes up a channel in the spine and You may experience that happening. Or want to imagine it happening.

But the important thing is for It to get there, and affirming that this is happening and imagining the

THE SOULFIRE MEDITATION

Soulfire already there is a much better way of getting the job done.

And don't be concerned about feeding the flame either. It still goes on in the background, even though You are no longer putting energy into It.

Begin with Your 2nd Center, drawing the Soulfire up as You breathe in and fanning Its flame as You breathe out. Do this three times, filling Your 2nd Center with the third inbreath which You then hold for three full counts of 4.

And remember that the best way to fan the flame is to breathe out strongly, almost explosively.

Bring the Soulfire to Your 3rd, 4th, 5th, 6th and 7th Centers in the same way, again holding the third inbreath for three full 4-counts and fanning the flame with each outbreath.

As you bring the Soulfire to Your 7th Center, allow any excess to flow out and down to its reservoir in Your 1st Center.

Complete this Step by again drawing the Soulfire up to Your 4th Center, going through the complete cycle three more times.

This is the first of the Soul Realization and Flowing Acceptance Centers, It's where It all starts, and It is therefore of special importance at this stage of Your growth.

TILLING THE SOUL

STEP 8 OF THE SOULFIRE MEDITATION

Affirming or asserting that something is true is a powerful tool for cultivating Soul Consciousness. It is an act of faith and inner knowing which You have been using regularly to reinforce each of the other Steps as You have taken them, but it is particularly important here in Step Eight, and in Step Nine.

In Step Seven You brought the Soulfire to the various Centers of Consciousness in turn, and now in Step Eight You affirm, as you fill each Center with the Soulfire, that You are also filling It with Its own particular quality of Soul Consciousness.

You start with Your 2nd Center, where the Soulfire is no longer blocked and the Creative Energy and Physical Vitality of this Center are now free to express themselves.

Then, as You bring the Soulfire to Your 3rd Center, which used to be the Emotion and Power Trip Center, You affirm that You are now filling It with Compassion and Quiet Strength.

THE SOULFIRE MEDITATION

Your 4th Center is where Soul Realization and Flowing Acceptance begin and as You bring the Soulfire to this Center, You affirm that You are filling It with **these** qualities.

As You bring the Soulfire to Your 5th Center, You affirm that You are filling It with **More** Soul Realization and **More** Flowing Acceptance.

And then, as You bring the Soulfire to Your 6th Center, You affirm that You are filling It with **Full** Soul Realization and **Full** Flowing Acceptance.

In other words, You are affirming that You are in the process of becoming a fully realized Soul, fully surrendered to the Unfolding Plan and fully committed to Its fulfillment.

As You fill Your 7th Center, You affirm that it is with Omega Realization and the many insights that this brings You.

And finally, as You go back to Your 4th Center, You affirm that You are filling It with the three most important aspects of Flowing Acceptance, first with Abiding Happiness, then with The Love That Passeth All Understanding, and finally with an Understanding of the Meaning and Purpose of Life.

Step Seven combined with Step Eight are the heart of the Soulfire Meditation and should be gone through twice before doing Step Nine.

TILLING THE SOUL

STEP 9 OF THE SOULFIRE MEDITATION

Step Nine of the Soulfire Meditation, the 10 Affirmations of Soul Consciousness, is a brief summary of truths and realizations that are already familiar to you.

The 1st Affirmation, "I Am a Soul, a Mind, a Consciousness, a Body of glowing, incandescent Light" and the first half of the 2nd Affirmation, "I Am both male and female, complete and whole within Myself", are part of Soul Realization.

The rest of the 2nd Affirmation, "Yet I Am joined in the most deeply intimate communion with every other Soul in the Cosmos" and the 3rd, "Omega, the One Soul, the One Mind, the One Consciousness became the Many and is now becoming the One again", and the 4th, "I Am becoming the One again", are part of Omega Realization.

The other 6 Affirmations, like "I Am just the way I need to be, just the way Omega needs to be, in Me as Me, to take the next step on My Path" and "Life is constantly providing Me with just what I need to experience, just what Omega needs to experience, along the way" are all part of Flowing Acceptance.

TILLING THE SOUL

The 10 Affirmations
of Soul Consciousness

I Am a Soul, a Mind, a Consciousness, a Body of
glowing, incandescent Light.

I Am both male and female, complete and whole
within Myself. Yet I am joined in the most deeply intimate
communion with every other Soul in the Cosmos.

Omega, the One Soul, the One Mind, the
one Consciousness, became the Many and is now
becoming the One again.

I Am becoming the One again.

Omega is Perfect, and I am part of Its Perfection.

I Am just the way I need to be, just the way
Omega needs to be, in Me as Me, to take the next step
on My Path.

TILLING THE SOUL

THE 10 AFFIRMATIONS OF SOUL CONSCIOUSNESS

I have just what I need to have, just what Omega
needs to have, to take that step.

And Life is constantly providing Me with just
what I need to experience, just what Omega needs
to experience, along the way.

There is only good. There is only Omega. Bad is
how I see those experiences whose part in my growth
I do not yet understand.

It is all part of the Plan, and I Am a Partner in Its
Unfolding.

STEP 10 OF THE SOULFIRE MEDITATION

Step Ten is Singing the Song of the Soul.

In the beginning was the Word. And the Word was a song. And the Song was OM.

There is only the One Soul. There is only the One Song. And only the One Voice Singing.

Yet the One Song is but the blending of all **our** melodies.

And the One Voice the sound of all **our** singings.

OM is the Song of Songs, the Song of the Soul.

And by adding Your OM to the OM of the Many, You will be attuning Your Soul vibration to the vibration of the One Soul. And of Oneness.

THE SOULFIRE MEDITATION

Just M-M-M a little at first to clear your throat. Then take a deep breath and exhale slowly and steadily, first sounding the letter O and then the letter M, like this, O-O-O-O-O-O-O-M-M-M-M-M-M-M, allowing about the same amount of breath for each letter.

As You continue to blend your OM with the OM of the Many, You will begin to feel a wonderful vibration going on inside You, especially inside Your head.

At the end, when You have finished singing Your song, sit quietly and experience the experience.

THE SOULFIRE
MEDITATION
CASSETTE

The Soulfire Meditation Cassette is designed to help you master the Soulfire Meditation more easily, and at the same time make It more rewarding and enjoyable and therefore easier to do regularly. And doing It every once in a while just isn't good for your growth.

The cassette begins with my voice gently guiding you through the first eight Steps of the Soulfire Meditation with words like "Bringing the Life Force to My 1st Center" and "Filling My 4th Center with Soul Realization and Flowing Acceptance" while bells toll softly in the background.

Then comes The Ten Affirmations of Soul Consciousness, which you say along with me if you wish, or repeat after me, or you can just sit and listen in your heart to the words and the very special music that accompanies them.

THE SOULFIRE MEDITATION CASSETTE

The cassette ends with the penetrating sound of over a hundred voices all OMing together and providing a very powerful vibration for your own OM to resonate with.

You can get one of these guided Soulfire Meditation Cassettes by sending a small contribution, five dollars is suggested, to The Communion of Souls, 372 Fifth Avenue, New York, N.Y. 10018.

The Communion
of Souls Meditation

There is a very special Meditation that we
practice here at the Communion of Souls, in addition
to doing the Soulfire Meditation on our own,
and if you would like to join us please contact me so
we can arrange to get together and talk about It.

Or, if you are too far away to come here to
meditate with us, you can always gather together a
group of kindred Spirits, Souls who share similar
truths and realizations and who practice the Soulfire
Meditation, and then, once you have done that, get in
touch with me and I will show you how you can have
your own Communion of Souls Meditation right
where you are.

TILLING THE SOUL

SOME REMINDERS AND A FEW SUGGESTIONS

Y ou now have proven Tools and Practices for growing Soul Consciousness but, like any other tools and practices, They aren't worth very much unless you use Them.

So begin experiencing more deeply. Live Your life more fully. Practice being in a here and now state of Meditation more and more of the time. This won't take away from anything else You are doing, it will only add to it.

Remember Your Breathing Meditation Practice and Your Walking Meditation Practice and any other Meditation Practices You have come up with.

And remember to Practice Being a Soul and
to Practice Flowing Acceptance.

None of these take time. Just attentiveness
and caring.

And above all remember to do Your Soulfire
Meditation.

Make It special. Have special pillows, for example,
and a special place to do It in.

If you have the Soulfire Meditation Cassette,
get a set of headphones to go with It. They cost as
little as five dollars and they will add a whole new
dimension to Your Meditation.

And do It at a special time. This makes it easier
for It to become a habit, something you do every day,
and finally a joyous necessity.

Right after getting up works best for me. The energy
is quieter then, there are fewer good excuses around,
and It's a great way to start the day.

If You can get someone else interested in the
Soulfire Meditation and can do It with them from time
to time, so much the better. Just sit facing each other
with Your eyes open, not looking **at** each other but
opening **to** each other. You will find that there is a

TILLING THE SOUL

different energy, a stronger energy this way that intensifies the Meditation for both of You and at the same time deepens Your feelings of Oneness.

All this sounds like a lot, doesn't it. But it really isn't, not if you take it one gradual step at a time.

And isn't it a relatively small price to pay for the Light of Soul Realization, the Joy of Abiding Happiness, the Love that Passeth all Understanding, and an Understanding of the True Meaning and Purpose of Your Life?

And once You have Them, once You feel Your Light and Love and Joy and Purpose burgeoning deep inside You, don't keep Them all for yourself or a special few but take Them out into the world with You and show Them forth to everyone.

And not just now and then, but in all Your doings throughout each day.

About Wingate

Wingate is an Ordained Minister, an Initiated Teacher who has lived and taught in an ashram, and the founder of The Communion of Souls.

A Mayflower New Englander with a family tradition of ministry, banking and the law and an honor graduate of Yale University, he was already a promising young executive for a major corporation when World War II began. And though partially blind in one eye, he joined the Marines and rose in rank to Captain.

Following the war, he left a future in business to become a highly-regarded photographer, culminating his career with a book of photographs that is considered a contemporary classic.

At the time when his ambitions had been handsomely achieved and his family was firmly secure, he found himself drawn into a spiritual quest. Over a period of nearly twenty years he would dramatically alter his lifestyle from that of a man of wealth and fame to that of a man of God and Service.

Tilling The Soul represents the essence of Wingate's philosophy and practices as a spiritual Teacher.

The Book of Surrender, also published by Aurora Press, is a series of twenty-two dramatic dialogues between Wingate and his beloved Teacher Emmanuel. It is a stirring story of his deepening consciousness in which cancer, a brain tumor and the ultimate lesson of surrender to the Will of God lead to his greater development as man and spiritual Teacher.

Ω

I am a Soul I am a Soul

I am a Soul I am a Soul I am a Soul I am a Soul I am a So
I am a Soul I am a Soul I am a Soul I am a Soul I am a S
l I am a Soul I am a Soul I am a Soul I am a Soul I am a S
ul I am a Soul I am a Soul I am a Soul I am a Soul I am a
oul I am a Soul I am a Soul I am a Soul I am a Soul I am
Soul I am a Soul I am a Soul I am a Soul I am a Soul I am
 Soul I am a Soul I am a Soul I am a Soul I am a Soul I a
a Soul I am a Soul I am a Soul I am a Soul I am a Soul I
 a Soul I am a Soul I am a Soul I am a Soul I am a Soul I
m a Soul I am a Soul I am a Soul I am a Soul I am a Soul
am a Soul I am a Soul I am a Soul I am a Soul I am a Soul
 am a Soul I am a Soul I am a Soul I am a Soul I am a Sou
I am a Soul I am a Soul I am a Soul I am a Soul I am a So
I am a Soul I am a Soul I am a Soul I am a Soul I am a S
l I am a Soul I am a Soul I am a Soul I am a Soul I am a
ul I am a Soul I am a Soul I am a Soul I am a Soul I am a
oul I am a Soul I am a Soul I am a Soul I am a Soul I am
Soul I am a Soul I am a Soul I am a Soul I am a Soul I am
 Soul I am a Soul I am a Soul I am a Soul I am a Soul I a
a Soul I am a Soul I am a Soul I am a Soul I am a Soul I
 a Soul I am a Soul I am a Soul I am a Soul I am a Soul I
m a Soul I am a Soul I am a Soul I am a Soul I am a Soul
am a Soul I am a Soul I am a Soul I am a Soul I am a Soul
 am a Soul I am a Soul I am a Soul I am a Soul I am a Sou
I am a Soul I am a Soul I am a Soul I am a Soul I am a So
I am a Soul I am a Soul I am a Soul I am a Soul I am a S
l I am a Soul I am a Soul I am a Soul I am a Soul I am a
ul I am a Soul I am a Soul I am a Soul I am a Soul I am a
oul I am a Soul I am a Soul I am a Soul I am a Soul I am
Soul I am a Soul I am a Soul I am a Soul I am a Soul I am
 Soul I am a Soul I am a Soul I am a Soul I am a Soul I a
a Soul I am a Soul I am a Soul I am a Soul I am a Soul I
 a Soul I am a Soul I am a Soul I am a Soul I am a Soul I
m a Soul I am a Soul I am a Soul I am a Soul I am a Soul
am a Soul I am a Soul I am a Soul I am a Soul I am a Soul
 am a Soul I am a Soul I am a Soul I am a Soul I am a Sou
I am a Soul I am a Soul I am a Soul I am a Soul I am a So
I am a Soul I am a Soul I am a Soul I am a Soul I am a S
l I am a Soul I am a Soul I am a Soul I am a Soul I am a
ul I am a Soul I am a Soul I am a Soul I am a Soul I am a
oul I am a Soul I am a Soul I am a Soul I am a Soul I am
Soul I am a Soul I am a Soul I am a Soul I am a Soul I am
 Soul I am a Soul I am a Soul I am a Soul I am a Soul I a
a Soul I am a Soul I am a Soul I am a Soul I am a Soul I
 a Soul I am a Soul I am a Soul I am a Soul I am a Soul I
m a Soul I am a Soul I am a Soul I am a Soul I am a Soul
am a Soul I am a Soul I am a Soul I am a Soul I am a Soul
 am a Soul I am a Soul I am a Soul I am a Soul I am a Sou
I am a Soul I am a Soul I am a Soul I am a Soul I am a So
I am a Soul I am a Soul I am a Soul I am a Soul I am a S
l I am a Soul I am a Soul I am a Soul I am a Soul I am a
ul I am a Soul I am a Soul I am a Soul I am a Soul I am a
oul I am a Soul I am a Soul I am a Soul I am a Soul I am
Soul I am a Soul I am a Soul I am a Soul I am a Soul I am
 Soul I am a Soul I am a Soul I am a Soul I am a Soul I